Looking for Your Next Job?

Work: Where to find it and how to get hired

Clive Lewis OBE DL

Cover design by Brendan Vaughan-Spruce

Also by the author

The Definitive Guide to Workplace Mediation and Managing Conflict at Work

Win Win – Resolving Workplace Conflict

Workplace Mediation skills – Training Handbook

Difficult Conversations – 10 Steps to Becoming a Tackler not a Dodger

Bouncing Back from Redundancy – 12 Steps to Get Your Career and Life Back on Track

Work-Life Balance – How to Put Work in its Place and Reclaim Your Life

Performance Management – Ten Steps to Getting the Most from Your Workforce

Difficult Conversations in Dementia – A Ten Step Toolkit for Clinicians Involved in End of Life Discussions

Leadership with Compassion – Applying Kindness, Dignity and Respect in Healthcare Management

Table of Contents

Looking for Your Next Job? Work: Where to find it and how to get
hired

Introduction

The world of work is an ever-evolving beast that reflects global trends as well as the desires and advancements of individual economies. In the UK, the gradual decline of production and manufacturing industries, coupled with the rise in technology firms and media services, has effected the biggest change in the world of work since the Industrial Revolution. This has had a well-publicised effect on employees in associated fields over recent decades, such as closures of mines, car plants and dockyards. Gone are the days when a single company or institution provided food for the tables of the majority of the local population. Add to this the very tangible impact of sudden recessions and the accompanying mass redundancies, and it quickly becomes clear that we as individuals have a duty to ensure that we are riding the waves of change rather than struggling to find a lifebelt when a storm hits.

Each month I receive emails and phone calls from professionals who wish to book a few hours of my time to talk about their next career move. This isn't because I have a sideline in career clairvoyance, but because they know I have vast experience in a range of industries, sectors and positions and am better placed than most to advise on decision making in terms of individual career goals. Throughout my career I have

The world of work is always evolving.

The UK has seen a gradual decline in production and manufacturing industries and a rise in technology firms and media services.

We as individuals have a duty to ensure that we are able to navigate a changing employment landscape rather than being left behind.

I frequently receive requests from individuals regarding their next career move.

experienced work at all levels, up to and including board level, in the private, public and voluntary sectors. I have been a full-time employee, a self-employed consultant and a non-executive director. I have also experienced redundancy. As you can see, my advice comes with experience to back it up! I decided to write this book off the back of these requests; combining my opinions with the latest thinking on the employment landscape; what changes we are likely to see in the foreseeable future; and, most importantly, how you as a driven, career-minded professional can adapt to these changes.

There are a number of statistics we can point to in order to emphasise the notion that the employment landscape is shifting, many of which are discussed in relevant chapters later in the book. However, it is important, before we begin, to illustrate just how common change is becoming within the global workforce. A good example of this is reflected in the average employee length of service and how it has changed in recent years.

In 2003, The Office for National Statistics published a report[1] comparing employment figures from 1996 and 2001, illustrating perfectly the way in which the attitude to work in the UK has changed and continues to change. An interesting finding was that in 1996 half of all employees had been working for the same firm

I have occupied many different positions in various sectors, from volunteer to board member, so my advice comes with weight.

This book combines my opinions with the latest thinking on the future of the employment landscape and how you can successfully navigate it.

A good example of a shift in employment landscape is that of employee length of service.

In 1996, the ONS found that half of all employees canvassed had been at the same firm for five years or less. By 2001, this had dropped to four years.

for five years or less. By 2001, it had dropped to four years. The trend for the younger generation to be more active job hoppers was also supported by the figures – only 51% of workers in the 18-24 age group were in the same job as 12 months previously compared with 86% of those aged 50 and over.

51% of workers in the 18-24 age bracket had been in the same job for 12 months, compared to 86% of those aged 50+.

Nine years down the line, in 2010, Gregg and Wadsworth found that 32% of 35-44 year old men were in jobs that had lasted for at least ten years compared to 49% of 55-64 year olds[2]. Contemporary generations of workers are realising that they have to constantly expand and refresh their skillset, and it is becoming increasingly apparent that employers are expecting new starters to remain with them for shorter and shorter periods and as a result find talent retention an increasing problem.

In 2010, a study found that 32% of 35-44 year old men were in jobs that had lasted for at least ten years compared to 49% of 55-64 year olds.

Change can be scary, especially for those who have been in a profession or industry for some time (employers are currently facing a labour market with fewer young people and more older employees), but organisations are faced with the constant issue of adapting to changing times or falling behind. This eventually impacts on all employees in one way or another. Those individuals who are proactive in their attitude towards change will ultimately fare better. This is why you have picked up this book.

Change can seem scary, but organisations are finding that they must adapt or fall behind, which leads to change for employees too.

A more proactive approach to change can greatly aid an individual's ability to deal with it.

And with that in mind, let us begin.

"We are all faced with a series of great opportunities brilliantly disguised as impossible situations."

Charles R Swindoll

"The readiness is all".

William Shakespeare

"Luck is what happens when preparation meets opportunity."

Seneca

Chapter 1 – Exploring the options

There may be numerous factors behind your desire to look for a new role. You may be looking for a different challenge, to learn something new, or to switch to an industry with more potential for growth. Alternatively, you may wish to work closer to home or take the pressure off and work part-time instead. Whatever your reasons for doing so, this first step is a great opportunity to take a step back and take a bird's eye perspective of your life; to remove the barrier between professional and personal and ask yourself where you would like your next steps to take you and what you really want out of life at this stage of your career. Would you like to earn more money, enjoy more security, or spend more time at home? Would you like to do something daring or exciting, or something that allows you to travel and broaden your experiences?

Financial considerations are naturally never far away from one's mind at this point, and rightly so. It may help to calculate your absolute minimum living requirements and then balance further earnings with your intentions in the work/life balance area. Again, this all depends on what your evaluated life goals are. For example, less pressure may mean less money but equal more family time. Which of these is really important to you? Making these evaluations will help you to manage your outgoings more effectively. Don't

There may be various reasons why you are looking to move on in your career, both personal and professional.

This first step is a great chance to take a step back and consider what you want out of life, and consequently your job – not the other way round.

Consider your priorities – do you prioritise money, progression, job security or time away from work, for example?

be afraid to be ruthless. Think of it as a business exercise. Every penny counts!

Personal options

As I have already mentioned, planning a career change, no matter how large or small, is a great opportunity to sit back and take stock of what you want out of life and assess whether anything needs changing. At this point, the changing world of work and all it encompasses needs to be set aside. The next stage will deal with this. That elusive work/life balance is something many of us fail to achieve properly, but this point in your plans is a good time to take steps towards achieving it. If you have a job that involves working long hours or weekends, do you mind this or would you prefer more leisure time? Do you see your family and friends as much as you wish? Do you want to work closer to home? Asking questions of this type may bring surprising answers and will immediately help you focus your search. Of course there may be factors in your life that mean change can't be facilitated wholesale (family responsibilities, travel costs etc.), but there are bound to be some areas for improvement. The opinions of others are always useful here if you think you're either stuck or, conversely, think you can now have the free and easy life!

Many of us neglect our work/life balance, but this is a great chance to assess yours.

Ask yourself some questions about your life outside of work – do you spend enough time with your friends, family or even yourself?

Consider what is important to you in terms of what life you would like your job/career to create for you.

Bear in mind that some factors will not be as flexible as others (salary, commuting time for example)

Employment options

When it comes to the types of work out there, your options are commonly divided into five sections. Generally speaking, these divisions aren't hugely affected by changes in industrial landscapes, although it is always wise to research the current/future prospects of those areas that particularly interest you.

Generally speaking, there are five types of work available.

The most common type of employment is **permanent** work. You will probably be familiar with permanent jobs, be they full-time or part-time. They are intended as long-term jobs with no pre-determined end date. They provide the most security, stability and regular income but bring with them a possible lack of variety and flexibility.

***Permanent work**: Full or part-time work with no pre-determined end date. **Pros**: Security, stability, regular income. **Cons**: Possible lack of variety and flexibility.*

Temporary, **contract** or **interim** work, either full-time or part-time, is work that carries with it a specific end date – although this can be extended or made permanent. People generally move from contract to contract every few months or have more than one going at once. Contract work provides more variety and a flexible working pattern, but brings with it a risk of periods of unemployment, irregular income and fewer benefits.

***Temp, contract or interim**: Full or part-time work with pre-determined end date (sometimes extendable). **Pros**: Variety, flexibility. **Cons**: Periods of unemployment, irregular income, fewer benefits.*

Self-employment is not for the faint-hearted. Many people like the idea of being their own boss but few realise what it actually entails. Running your own business can be immensely satisfying and can be

***Self-employment**: Running your own business, from consultancy to franchise.*

achieved in almost any field you choose, from consultancy work to running a franchise to being a plumber. It offers independence, job satisfaction, flexibility and potentially high earnings but demands very hard work with the risk of little initial reward, loss of security and benefits (pension, legal rights, paid holiday) and potential isolation for long periods.

A combination of different roles such as part-time positions, self-employment or voluntary work, is known as a **portfolio career**. They are increasing in popularity and offer variety, flexibility and the chance to broaden your skill base but carry with them irregular income, lack of security and loss of traditional rights and benefits.

Alternative lifestyles will suit far less people than the previous areas outlined, but for those in a position to accept, they can be the most satisfying. Alternative lifestyles can involve public appointments (sitting on advisory bodies, tribunals or public corporations), or voluntary work. Many find the challenge, the personal reward, the independence and the opportunity to grow enjoyable, but beware the time required to achieve your new goals, the loss of earnings and the odd hours.

As well as the types of work available, it is also worth analysing the two sectors in which employment falls – **public** or **private**. Naturally some jobs will immediately

Pros: Independence, job satisfaction, flexibility, potential high earnings. Cons: Hard work, little initial reward, loss of rights/benefits.

Portfolio career: Combination of different roles. Pros: Variety, flexibility, chance to broaden skillset. Cons: Irregular income, lack of security, loss of rights/benefits

Alternative: Public appointments, voluntary/non-paid work. Pros: Challenge, personal reward, independence, chance to grow. Cons: Odd hours, loss of earnings, time required to achieve goals.

decide this for you as far as this goes (e.g. investment banker, council administrator), but a change of sector may be something you hadn't considered although may like the idea of. It is worth researching the pros and cons of both before making a decision however, as the appeal may be different from the reality! There is indeed the option of taking some time out totally and volunteering in the third sector, however, I won't be covering this in detail in this book, given that the majority of people will be interested in paid employment.

The following chapters explore three very important areas when it comes to planning your next career move – the industries of the future, skills and mindset – and marrying up these aspects with all of the options and ideas above should give you a very clear idea of what you want out of life and your next job – something you probably haven't had the chance to do for a while.

*Consider a change of sector (**public** or **private**) for a different challenge.*

If you fancy a change in this area, try to speak to those working in that arena as the reality may be different from the perceived reality!

"Job security is gone. The driving force of a career must come from the individual."

Hama Bahrami

"It is not the strongest of the species that survive, nor the most intelligent, but the one most responsive to change."

Charles Darwin

"It is extremely unlikely that anyone coming out of school with a technical degree will go into one area and stay there. Today's students have to look forward to the excitement of probably three or four careers."

Gordon Moore

Chapter 2 – The industries of the future

This chapter looks at the two ends of the industrial growth scale – declining and growing industries. Many of us will be aware of some if not all of the declining industries, but some of the industries predicted to grow might come as a surprise.

It is important to see what has happened to industry in order to predict future patterns.

Declining Industries

To get a good idea of where industry is going, it is important to see where it has been and where it is at present. The following chart, provided by the CIPD[3], gives a great overview of this story by virtue of the composition of employment in British industry between 1841-2011:

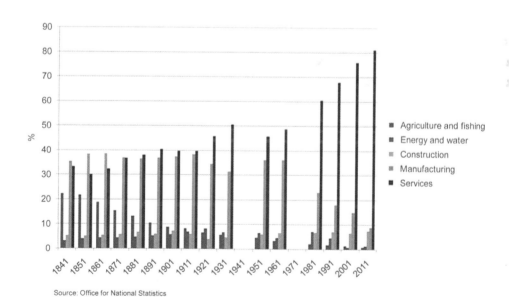

Source: Office for National Statistics

It doesn't take a statistician to identify the trends of the last seventy years, or to recognise that the type of labour-intensive manufacture that formed Britain's industrial spine in the 1800s, has now relocated to emerging markets where labour and materials are cheaper – most notably the Far East. It also shouldn't need me to advise you not to consider careers in the worst performing industries.

Labour intensive manufacture has left the UK and relocated to emerging markets – most notably the Far East.

Allied to the information above, reputable research body IBISWorld have outlined three sectors that have been in decline since 2011 and which they believe may still be in decline by end of the decade[4-5]. Despite being a US survey, very similar patterns can be seen already across most first world countries.

IBISWorld outlined three sectors that have been in decline in the US since 2011:

1. Manufacture: This sector is not in decline because we desire fewer products but because manufacturers are shifting their production overseas to capitalise on cheaper labour and technological advances. Manufacture of apparel and hardware are predicted to be the biggest losers in this industry by 2017. Allied to this, appliance repair has also seen a huge decline with people frequently preferring to buy new appliances rather than have existing ones repaired.

Manufacture: Overseas production has utilised cheap labour and technological advances.

Appliance repair has also dipped as people prefer to buy rather than repair.

2. Retail: The death of the high street is not a new concept to most of us, and IBISWorld predicts that it isn't about to get better – quite the reverse in fact, with huge declines seen in bricks and mortar

Retail: The high street is a tough place to be right now, and it isn't about to get better.

establishments in recent years (2011 saw a 76% decline in the revenues of US record shops, for example). The explosion and continued rise of digital media and internet shopping has meant that the profits of high street retail stores are only expected to head in one direction.

The rise of digital media and online shopping has exacerbated this decline.

3. Information: In 2011, IBISWorld found that a huge number of industries within the information sector were in decline. By 2012, some industries had reversed the overall trend (VoIP, ISPs, search engines and software publishers grew), but troubles still lie ahead for the wired telecommunications industry; the DVD, game and video rental industry; the newspaper publishing industry; the photofinishing industry; and the recordable media industry.

Information: A number of industries in this sector have struggled and are expected to continue to struggle, mainly those who have found digital information replacing physical.

These are not death sentences of course, but it is certainly worth considering whether a change of direction into one of these sectors is the best thing for your future.

Growing Industries

Of course, no one can predict the future of employment (no one in 2007 could have predicted what would happen to the economy the following year), but it is possible to analyse world trends to calculate, with a degree of accuracy, which jobs and industries are likely to be in demand in the next five to ten years. The continual infiltration of technology into all aspects of our lives for example, or the steadily rising ageing population, aren't going to alter too significantly (barring a global catastrophe) and so jobs associated with these industries are as safe a bet as one can make.

We can predict reasonably well which industries will grow in the coming years.

The following ten industries are those predicted by IBISWorld and the Bureau of Labor Statistics (BLS) to be the top ten flourishing industries in 2020[6]. Again, although they are focused on the US economy, similar changes can already be seen in most major economies.

IBISWorld and the BLS predict the following industries to be flourishing in 2020:

1. **Data analysis:** Data is everywhere – every click of our mouse or swipe of our finger is recorded somewhere by somebody and is made useful by data analysts on behalf of companies (or indeed governments) eager to cash in on these mountains of information. Those with the ability to make sense of these numbers and turn them into useful, actionable information will be incredibly valuable.

Data analysis: As data gathering grows (both by governments and organisations) so will opportunities for those who can decipher it and make it actionable.

2. **Counselling and therapy:** The knowledge that mental health is equally as important as physical health, especially in such a chaotic world, is expected to lead to a growth in demand for professionals in this field. The BLS expects the biggest growing area for counsellors and therapists to be in the marriage and family field, where they anticipate growth of 41 percent by 2020.

Counselling and therapy: Mental health is in the public domain more and more. As discussing it becomes less taboo and more people seek help, therapists and counsellors will be in demand.

3. Scientific research: If you thought all the breakthroughs in science had been made, think again! Biologists, chemists, mathematicians and engineers will all be sought after in the coming years, with particular growth expected in the fields of biotechnology, biomedicine, nanotechnology, robotics and 3D printing.

4. Computer engineering: Faster is better, so we are led to believe, and the continuing desire to develop faster and more efficient software, not to mention the growing desire for bespoke software, requires computer experts to bring these elements together. As long as business grows and diversifies, this industry will be required to help them do so.

5. Veterinarians: We love our pets; the BLS expects the need for vets to rise 36 percent by 2020. Advances in treatment are expected to lead to veterinary care that rivals human healthcare by this time.

6. Environmental and conservation science: This industry, and the global issues that warrant its expansion, have been making headlines for decades. Yet scientific advancements have meant, and will continue to mean, that we are finally able to make much better use of the Earth's natural resources as a continually rising global population slowly drains what natural materials remain. Green energy, despite some political controversy, still seems likely to boom.

Scientific research: Biologists, chemists, mathematicians and engineers will all be sought after in the coming years, as well as those knowledgeable in the technologies of the future.

Computer engineering: The desire to build complex bespoke systems is growing. Somebody needs to build these systems, and fix them.

Veterinarians: the BLS expects the need for vets to rise 36 percent by 2020 as treatment rivals human care.

Environmental and conservation science: Ecology is a booming industry, with the importance of renewable energy and mitigating/reversing global warming increasing in importance.

7. Some healthcare fields: An ageing, and growing, population will lead to increased demands on healthcare by 2020. Some jobs in healthcare tend to be low paying, but this is offset by the perceived immunity to recessions within some aspects of the sector. Demand is expected to be strong for nurses, optometrists, audiologists, dentists and therapy.

Some healthcare fields: Demand is expected in the fields of nursing, optometry, audiology, dentistry and therapy.

8. Management: Effective management is expected to have shifted its focus by 2020, requiring basic business knowledge plus the ability to oversee operations in many locations and countries, and some technical know-how. The ability to effectively manage people is a skill that will always be in demand, especially someone who can combine this with the ability to handle the proliferation of technology in their chosen profession.

Management: Management will be much more than managing people in 2020, with the emphasis also on the ability to handle technology too.

9. Finance: The world of banking and high finance hasn't exactly been out of the news in recent years. Yet, rather than the return of multinational banking empires it is the smaller non-traditional investment firms such as hedge funds and private equity firms that are expected to grow as the traditional banking sector complies with new regulations and reins in its risk-taking. This increases the demand for finance experts, a demand which may not be met as students once interested in finance turn to other industries following

Finance: Non-traditional investment firms such as hedge funds and private equity firms are expected to grow rather than traditional baking.

16

the 2008 financial crash and the associated stigma of the industry.

10. Entrepreneurship: The explosion in the app creation industry has opened up the possibility of entrepreneurship to anyone with a computer, an idea, and the desire to see it through; some making millionaires of their creators almost overnight. Similarly, self-publishing in the literary and music industries has allowed writers and musicians alike to create, market and sell their own products. Interestingly, however, it is in traditional businesses such as used-car dealers, hair and nail salons, pet grooming and office services where forecasters predict the biggest growth. It could be, however, that another Facebook, Twitter or iPad blows everything out of the water and starts another cultural snowball rolling. Could that idea be yours?

Again, it is important to state that these are just predictions based on current and anticipated trends, but many of these predictions can already be seen in the marketplace. A British equivalent was offered by the CIPD[3] who analysed employment composition in the UK and found that between 1978 and 2013 the greatest increases in employment came in the following sectors:

Entrepreneurship: It is easier than ever in this digital world to create and sell something. Overnight success stories are not unknown, although traditional small businesses and services are expected to flourish more.

These are just predictions based on current and anticipated trends, but many of these predictions can already be seen in the marketplace.

- Real estate (employment up 205%)
- Professional, scientific and technical activities (up 169%)
- Administrative and support services (up 139%)
- Health-related activities (up 113%)

You can see the similarities between the BLS/IBISWorld research and this; with the findings of this research also tying in with the suggestion that skilled service-based jobs are replacing less skilled, more labour-intensive ones.

It is worth spending a little time considering if any of these growing industries appeals to you and researching the current employment opportunities within them to give you an idea of the kind of positions and skills required. If you don't fancy any of these industries then it may be more constructive to move onto the next chapter which focuses on your personal skillset.

Take a little time considering if any of these growing industries interests you and research the roles within them and the skills required.

"The most effective way to cope with change is to help create it."

L.W. Lynett

"There are times in everyone's life when something constructive is born out of adversity...when things seem so bad that you've got to grab your fate by the shoulders and shake it."

Author unknown

"If we don't change, we don't grow. If we don't grow, we are not really living."

Lord Chesterfield

Chapter 3 – Adapting your skillset & lifelong learning

With the changes we are experiencing in the job market, there has never been a better time to focus on lifelong learning. The desire and drive to constantly evolve one's learning is crucial to continued success – companies such as Google, Apple and Gillette are always looking for new avenues to explore and new technologies to exploit. Missed opportunities can cost billions.

Learning should never stop. The most successful companies are those that continue to search for new avenues and learn about new technologies.

Lifelong learning is just as important for individuals; those who stop learning and exploring new opportunities limit the directions that life can take them and can lend themselves a disadvantage as far as continued employment goes. I once spoke on this topic at a conference for education professionals, and in preparing my speech I thought of my own previous learning and classroom exercises that looked at various PEST models. PEST normally stands for Political, Economic, Social and Technical, but with a few amendments to the original model here is a PEST framework that supports lifelong learning.

When we stop learning ourselves we limit the directions in which life can take us.

Personal – Learning brings personal confidence and growth. Absorbing new information and facts and maintaining awareness of developments in these areas allows us to be better able to engage in dialogue and put our opinions across on a wider variety of topics. This also has the added benefit of making us seem,

Personal benefits: learning brings confidence and growth, allowing us to actively engage on a variety of topics.

rightly or not, to be more intelligent, and thus become more respected – someone people go to on certain matters.

Economic: Across the developed world, and the political spectrum, everybody agrees about the importance of education. It is good for society, which needs the contributions and economic productivity – not to mention the tax – of a skilled workforce, and it is good for individuals. People with a higher standard of education earn more, are more satisfied with their work and leisure time, are less likely to be unemployed, unhealthy or take part in criminal activity. Furthermore, they are more likely to volunteer their time and vote in elections. According to the US Department of Labor, a student who went to high school but didn't graduate with a diploma earned an average of $419 per week. This sum rose to $595 for those who had graduated with a diploma, $1,039 for those who had gone on to college and earned a bachelor's degree, and $1,200 for those with an advanced degree[7].

Economic benefits: learning and education benefits the economy in a number of ways, from taxation on higher salaries to raised revenue from improved business.

Social: When people are engaged in learning, there is a high likelihood that dependency on organisations such as Social Services will reduce or be completely eliminated, which is of huge benefit to the country in a variety of ways. A more educated society also leads to a more cordial, responsible and understanding society.

Social benefits: a more educated society is often a more cordial and responsible society. Reliance on state handouts is also reduced.

Tactical: Continued learning can help put the building blocks in place to move from one role to another. If you have identified an area of work that you would like to engage in but are not quite ready for, learning can help bridge the gap to get you the role you have your eye on.

Tactical benefits: further learning can bridge gaps in knowledge to allow you to move from one job to another or progress in an existing role.

Lifelong learning can therefore enrich our lives both professionally and personally. Learning about other cultures, for example, can make us more informed when it comes to dealing with foreign clients or customers, whilst learning a foreign language is known to increase employment options. Continual learning is also an important feature of later life; regular mental stimulation keeps the brain active and can, according to research, aid memory and help stave off illnesses such as dementia and Alzheimer's.

Continual learning can enrich our lives both professionally and socially. Learning a foreign language for example can both widen our scope for potential employment and open up new social avenues.

There are countless ways in which continual learning will help you grow, both professionally and personally. Whichever way you choose to do it, prospective employers will be impressed that you have used your resources, both in terms of time and perhaps capital, to ensure that you are proactive in not only evolving your education but also the fact that you can do so quickly and effectively. In the same way that banks look more favourably on those who have taken out and repaid loans than those who have never borrowed in their lives, some employers will favour candidates who

Employers will be impressed that you have used your redundancy time and money to widen your learning – make sure you mention it.

have triumphed over adversity than those who have never faced it.

Desirable skills

A key question we are concerned with is, of course, what skills the changing employment landscape will demand. In 2011, the Institute for the Future (working out of the University of Phoenix Research Institute) released a report entitled 'Future Work Skills 2020', which forecast the ten most important skills for the future workforce[8]. These were:

A key issue is what skills will be desirable in the future workforce.

- **Sense making** - ability to determine the deeper meaning or significance of what is being expressed.

- **Social intelligence** - ability to connect to others in a deep and direct way, to sense and stimulate reactions and desired interactions.

- **Novel and adaptive thinking** - proficiency at thinking and coming up with solutions and responses beyond that which is route or rule-based.

- **Cross cultural competency** - ability to operate in different cultural settings.

- **Computational thinking** - ability to translate vast amounts of data into abstract concepts and to understand data-based reasoning.

- **New media literacy** - ability to critically assess and develop content that uses new media forms, and to leverage these media for persuasive communication.

- **Transdiciplinarity** - literacy in and ability to understand concepts across multiple disciplines.

- **Design mindset** - ability to represent and develop tasks and work processes for desired outcomes.

- **Cognitive load management** - ability to deconstruct and filter information for importance, and to understand how to maximize cognitive functioning using a variety of tools and techniques.

- **Virtual collaboration** - ability to work productively, drive engagement, and demonstrate presence as a member of a virtual team.

These suggestions are based on current trends and predicted growth, but, like the industry example, some of these skills are already organically developing in certain workforces and are already being sought by employers.

It may help to research the jobs or career opportunities that interest you to see which of these skills are already sought after.

With this information in mind, it may help to research the career opportunities that interest you to see which of these skills are already sought after. Which ones do you already possess and which could you do with brushing up on? Of course your ideal job may not require all of the skills listed, but it nevertheless helps to provide an overall view here of what will likely be demanded of the future workforce.

Your ideal job may not need all of these desired skills, but it helps to see what skills are expected to be in demand.

Equally as important as skills, and in fact more important according to many, is the mindset and personal character traits of the future workforce. This area is discussed in the following chapter.

"Our progress as a nation can be no swifter than our progress in education."

John F. Kennedy

"Get over the idea that only children should spend their time in study. Be a student so long as you still have something to learn, and this will mean all your life."

Henry L. Doherty

"I don't think much of a man who is not wiser today than he was yesterday."

Abraham Lincoln.

Chapter 4 – Mindset

In a world of qualifications, training and transferable skills, it is easy to become confused as to what employers really want now, or will want in the future. According to a 2011 survey by national recruitment consultancy firm Reed, 96% of the 1,263 organisations questioned said they would rather hire someone without the complete skillset but with the right mindset over the alternative[9]. So if skills alone won't get you the job, what will? What is it that employers are looking for?

It's not just skills that employers want – they want to know that you have the drive and desire to do the job too.

The answer is 'values' – the core traits that come together to make up an individual's attitude to their work. Employers are looking for candidates with the right skillset *and* the right mindset – in other words they want someone with the tools to do the job and the drive to get it done on time and professionally. These values are explored here.

Many employers hold these character traits, or values, in higher esteem than an employee's skill set, including 96% of over 1,000 organisations recently surveyed.

Most importantly to employers is a **strong work ethic**. This doesn't just mean working hard, it also means working smart. Prospective employers will want to see that you have the drive to see tasks through to the end, that you take pride in what you do and that you work intelligently and within constraints of time and money. Try to think of examples when you have shown dedication towards a task above and beyond what was expected of you.

Employers will want to be sure that you have a strong work ethic. This means not just that you work hard but that you work smart too. Try to think of examples that display both.

Linked to work ethic is **teamwork** – an essential value in almost any workplace, in any industry. Individuals who can demonstrate that they are team players, that they are prepared to offer support, receive advice and work with their team to achieve common goals, will be highly regarded. It may be a cliché to say that you are a team player, but it is an important one to remember and demonstrate.

Teamwork is also a crucial value for the modern day worker to possess. Recalling an experience where teamwork helped solve a problem or complete a difficult task will demonstrate your abilities in this area.

Employers will also want to be sure of your **dependability and responsibility**. They will want to know that you will be somewhere when you say you'll be there and that you won't shirk from the responsibility of your position when things get difficult or if you fall behind schedule. This relates back to basic issues of trust, the foundations upon which all relationships are built. Try and demonstrate instances where you were in a position of trust and responsibility, ideally ones in which you volunteered your efforts.

Employers will need to know that you are dependable and reliable. They will want to know that you can be trusted to carry out your duties honestly and to the best of your ability, but that you will ask for help if you need it.

Those with a **positive attitude** are also favoured by employers, perhaps for obvious reasons; someone with a positive attitude will approach a problem and see how it can be overcome, whereas someone with a negative attitude might let the first setback be the last. Try to demonstrate instances when you have overcome a series of issues on the way to successfully tackling a problem.

Employers like positive attitudes. Make sure that when you approach potential employers you are keen, enthusiastic and confident about taking on challenges.

Professionalism is also a key value employers look for. Professionals look, dress and speak in a manner reflecting their profession, company and personal pride. Clients and customers expect to be dealt with in a professional manner, so make sure you treat potential employers in the way you would treat clients and customers.

Employers also demand professionalism. They want to know that you will be a good ambassador for the company. Make sure the way you look, dress and act match the requirements of the company.

Other values to consider putting across to prospective employers include: adaptability, self-motivation, self-confidence, desire for personal growth and loyalty. Be careful not to reel off this entire list of values in an interview. Instead, drop them into the conversation as appropriate and always try to back them up with examples if you can. Hopefully a combination of directly relevant skills and a broad base of core values will make you the perfect candidate.

Also, consider mentioning your adaptability, self-motivation, self-confidence, desire for personal growth and loyalty – but not all at the same time. Drop them into conversation where relevant.

Another study that reinforced the idea of traits and values being more important than skills was conducted in 2011 by IBM[10]. They questioned 1,709 CEOs around the world and asked them what they looked for when recruiting staff. The results were, in order of importance:

1. Collaborative
2. Communicative
3. Creative
4. Flexible
5. Opportunity seeking

As the results show, the CEOs put character traits above any individual skills in terms of importance to them and the success of their organisations. Looking at those traits, it is hard to believe that they have altered hugely in the last ten to fifteen years or are likely to change in the near future, unless there is a seismic shift in industry. When combined with the findings of the previous two chapters, we are gaining a clearer picture of the variables that will make up the future workforce, some of which may appeal to you more than others.

These traits are unlikely to change in the near to middle future.

The next part of the book tackles the practical aspect of moving on in your career, so you might like to pause here and, if you haven't already, research potential jobs, career options or industries using the information provided in the first four chapters.

"It is a thousand times better to have common sense without education than to have an education without common sense".

Robert G Ingersoll

"Be careful how you think. Your life is shaped by your thoughts."

Proverbs 4 v 23

"If you aren't fired with enthusiasm, you will be fired with enthusiasm."

Vince Lombardi

Chapter 5 – The visible job market

The visible job market is the one we all know – external advertisements (newspapers, internet etc.), recruiters (head-hunters and agencies) and online jobsites. The advantage to these visible methods is that the role, requirements and salary are all known up front, but the disadvantage is that thousands or even millions of people may be pursuing the same avenue.

The visible job market consists of advertised jobs, recruiters and online jobsites.

The process for applying for **advertised jobs** varies but should be clearly stated on each advert. As with any type of submission, ensure that your CV and covering letter are tailored for each individual job you apply for. This may seem like a laborious process, but with so many people applying for jobs you need to tick as many boxes as possible – something that can only be achieved if you directly match up your skills and experiences with the unique requirements of each job. A little effort here can bring a lot of reward whilst laziness or lack of attention to detail can be costly.

We are all familiar with advertised jobs in their various forms – be they in newspapers and journals or online. Ensure that your CV and covering letter are tailored for each job application.

Before leaping into a decision to apply for a job, ensure you have clearly read and understood the specifications of the role – including reading between the lines. Some recruiters may try to camouflage less desirable elements of the job, so be careful. If possible, speak to the recruiter before applying. This could be a genuine call to confirm details about the job spec, but don't let a lack of questions hold you back; find a

Ensure you read and understand the job spec before applying. Some unscrupulous advertisers may try to camouflage undesirable elements of the job.

reason to call them and do so. The aim here is to plant a seed in the recruiter's head of how keen, professional and genuine you sound on the phone so that when your CV comes through they remember you. An initial polite, pleasant and professional phone call may just bump you up the list a little. At any rate, it's worth a try.

Find an excuse to call the recruiter so they can get a better feel for who you are. Hopefully they'll remember you when your CV comes through.

A second side to the visible market is the world of **recruitment agencies**. Agencies in various markets have boomed in recent years, with the result that competition in many parts of the country is cut-throat. This competition is of major benefit to you as a candidate, given that consultants often have great recruitment networks and earn their living by getting people like you jobs. There are three types of recruiter, all of which work slightly differently.

There are now agencies for almost every area of work, from junior to senior positions. This competitive market is great for candidates.

High street agencies tend to work with more junior roles and match up candidates they think can be placed with existing vacancies that have to be filled. You walk into the branch or register on their website, the recruiter determines whether they think they can place you before registering you and you go from there. It is common practice to call an agency once a week or so if you haven't heard from them, just to remind them that you're still looking, but don't bombard them. Remember – they make money from getting you a job, so they will be looking.

High street agencies usually work with more junior roles.

Registering with more than one agency is advisable, but always be honest with them about your job hunt developments.

Head-hunters use company briefs to search the market for suitable candidates. They use their contacts and researchers to identify targets which they then present to the client to choose from. Approaching a head-hunter yourself will occasionally yield results, but, due to the nature of their work, they will often turn down applicants. If you are of a senior level, making head-hunters in your chosen sphere aware of your skills and availability might not be a bad idea – assuming that you want to stay in that field. The reality is, if you are making an impact (or have made one) in your organisation and particularly your industry, it is likely that some may already be aware of you.

Head-hunters recruit for more senior roles and will usually find you rather than you approaching them. If you are of a senior level however, it can't hurt to make head-hunters in relevant industries aware of your position.

Selection consultants receive a brief from a company, create a person specification and job advertisement and then publish them on appropriate websites or in appropriate publications. They then collate the best applicants, shortlist them and present them to the company for final selection. As the description suggests, you may only ever come into contact with them through adverts.

Selection consultants work on company briefs to come up with a person specification and a job advert, which they then place, filter candidates and present a shortlist to the client.

Finally, **jobsites** are online mediums where jobseekers upload their CVs for recruiters to search and respond to recruiter adverts. There are specialist jobsites and generalist jobsites, so make sure you choose carefully and, again, tailor your CV accordingly. Treat your online profile professionally (i.e. no silly photos) and don't be

Jobsites are an online medium where recruiters and candidates can register, interact and post/apply for jobs.

afraid to contact registered businesses you like the look of. After all, they're on the site for a reason.

Treat your online profile with as much professionalism as your other communications with potential employers. And don't be scared to contact those you like the look of either.

"Keep asking until you find the answers. In sales there are usually four or five 'no's' before you get a 'yes'.

Jack Cranfield

"When defeat comes, accept it as a signal that your plans are not sound, rebuild those plans, and set sail once more toward your coveted goal".

Napoleon Hill

"Perseverance is the hard work you do after you get tired of doing the hard work you already did".

Newt Gingrich

Chapter 6 – The hidden job market

Estimates suggest that some 80% of jobs are not advertised, which is incredible when you consider that national recruitment agencies often feature hundreds of thousands of jobs at one time. So how do you get access to these 'hidden' jobs? Sadly there is no easy answer, but the secret lies with being proactive in your approach, using your network of friends, clients and colleagues and contacting companies directly.

Some 80% of jobs are not advertised. The rest are filled through existing contacts, direct approaches and internal promotions.

Networking is the most common method of obtaining jobs in the hidden market. Networking success can sometimes come down to the personality of the individual – some find it natural and some find it difficult – but once you know the dos and don'ts and meet with the odd success or two you will think nothing of it.

Networking is the best way to crack the hidden market. You don't have to have high-powered contacts, but you should be aware of who best to approach and how to do so.

Once you have assessed your options and chosen your career direction using the steps outlined previously, head to your address book or handheld device and identify around ten desirable contacts.

Once you have identified your first round of contacts, it's time to approach them. Your method of contact will depend on the type of relationship you have – phone calls are suitable for closer relationships but you will probably find yourself emailing more than phoning. There are a couple of rules you should abide by in

Identify around ten 'first choice' contacts and approach them regarding their thoughts on what you should do or where you should go. Avoid asking them directly if they know of positions available.

order to make your canvassing as successful as possible. Firstly, don't ask for a job directly. This may make the conversation somewhat awkward as your contact may feel like you are just using them to look for work. Make it clear that you are only seeking advice and information as to your next steps and who it may be worth contacting, not job hunting directly.

The chances of getting a job directly off the back of these initial calls are limited, but you may be given referrals to those who may be able to help. Follow these referrals up within a few days with a written introduction, again making clear that you are only after information and advice. Outlining your strengths, qualities and experience and asking what this new contact might suggest is a very good way of discreetly advertising yourself to them. Don't be tempted to send in your CV unless requested – this will put you firmly in the 'job hunting' camp. There is no harm in following up emails after a week if you have received no reply, but don't hassle them. They are doing you a favour after all. If you strike it lucky and a contact comes good then the standard recruitment wheels will get into motion from there, meaning it's time to work on your CV and interviewing skills (see later steps).

The other approach to breaking into the hidden market is **direct contact**. This is the 'cold-calling' side of the recruitment world, and as such takes more time, effort

Consider carefully whether emailing or phoning is the best means of initial contact.

The most likely outcome is that you will be given another name to contact. Follow this up within a few days.

Again, don't be obvious but mention your strengths and experience and ask their advice. This is a discreet form of self-promotion.

Follow up unanswered emails or unreturned calls after a few days, but remember that they are doing you a favour so don't hassle them.

and luck than using existing networks. However, the right approach at the right time may pay dividends.

To begin with, put together a list of companies you would like to work for and whom you suspect may at some point have opportunities that would suit your experience, direction and skillset. Research these companies as much as possible to find any recent contracts they may have won, new offices they may have opened or have planned, even any departures that may have made the news. Essentially, try and find any potential gap in the company that you feel you could fill. If you find something appropriate, mention this specifically in your approach letter. If not, don't worry.

Direct contact means sending your CV and covering letter to companies direct. It requires more time and effort and positive results are fewer than using contacts, but you only need to be lucky once.

Research the company, find the name of the person who deals with recruitment in the area you want to target and send them your CV and covering letter (see step 8 for more details on this). If you don't hear anything back within a week, follow-up with a phone call to see if the letter was received and if there is anything suitable on the horizon. If you are told there are no vacancies, ask how you should find out about vacancies in the future and if you can be kept on file. Keep a note of the name of this person – people change jobs, and a phone call a matter of weeks down the line may yield a different name of someone who won't be aware of you, thus allowing you to try again.

Remember that people change jobs, so the person you contact may not be in that position in a few weeks' time. This means you can try again.

There is no winning formula to approaching companies directly. The secret is thorough research, a professional approach and a bit of fortunate timing. If they have something for you, great. If not, move on to the next company. Don't get downbeat at rejections and lack of contact – just keep plugging away. Luck is often no more than the product of hard work and persistence.

Luck can play a part in the success of direct contacting, but persistence and hard work will increase your chances of a lucky break

"It's all about people, it's about networking and being nice to people and not burning any bridges...in the end it is people that are going to hire you."

Mike Davidson

"It isn't just what you know, and it isn't just who you know. It's actually who you know, who knows you, and what you do for a living."

Bob Burg

"If you are not moving closer to what you want in sales (or in life), you probably aren't doing enough asking."

Jack Cranfield

Chapter 7 – Best practice

Dealing with two job markets, dozens of application forms, numerous CVs and various recruiters will inevitably lead to mistakes. Some mistakes are small and largely inconsequential, but many of the bigger ones are easily avoided.

When dealing with so many people, communications and businesses, you will undoubtedly make mistakes. You can, however, make life much easier for yourself in a number of ways.

The first mistake many people make is blanket applications. You may think that registering with multiple agencies, applying for any and all jobs in your salary bracket and firing off CVs to all the companies in your postal code may increase your chances of success. In fact the reverse is often true. Of course your chances of getting an interview are higher, but the risks of confusion, multiple interviews and agency suspicion mean that clashing or even missed appointments are increasingly likely. There is also the risk of having too many interviews to handle at one time, meaning that you may spread yourself too thin, scrimp on research and interview badly. This lack of research can manifest itself even if you are successful at an interview and get a job – you may fail to ask key questions or understand the role properly. Result? You quickly become unhappy and want to leave. Blanket applications also usually means the cardinal sin of sending untailored CVs and covering letters is committed on a frequent basis.

Don't be tempted to blanket apply for jobs. This will likely lead to untailored CVs and covering letters going to a multitude of companies with no strategy in place.

Canvassing too many companies at once can lead to confusion, mistakes and a lack of adequate research.

Instead of this saturation approach, use your personal and professional ambitions and your chosen industrial sectors to search for jobs you know you want and will do well in. You can always alter your expectations and required salary and widen your field of search if you meet with no success, but starting off in this manner will often produce much more satisfactory results.

Use your revised career goals to identify companies and industries you want to work for. You can always alter your expectations later.

As we have seen, employment agencies can be useful given their contacts and experience, but many people register with upwards of four at a time – sometimes lying if they are asked that exact question by the next in line. Employment agencies can be jealous beasts and don't like it if you register with competitors without telling them. It is of general courtesy to inform them of any relevant change in your circumstances – a courtesy which will be rewarded when they speak to companies on your behalf. Give them something good to say. Try and stick to a maximum of four agencies at one time, but equally don't feel under pressure to accept the first job they offer you. They want to make a sale after all, and some less scrupulous ones may try and squeeze you in anywhere to get their commission. Stick to your guns and they'll soon get the message.

Avoid registering with more than four agencies at once to avoid confusion and potential overburden.

Inform agencies if you have registered with a competitor and remain courteous even if they haven't found you any jobs. Give them good things to say about you.

Don't feel under pressure to accept the first job an agency offers you. They want to make a sale after all. Stick to your career goals until you feel the time may be right to accept a different role.

Many people also become unstuck through poor planning; they fire off letters to various companies without tracking what they have sent to whom and when, so when it comes to chasing up time, their records are a mess and they end up calling some people twice and forgetting others. Simply keeping a track of what was sent to whom, when, and what progress was made, will allow you to easily track any follow-up calls you need to make and will eliminate the risk of over calling and forgetting.

A mistake many people make that severely hampers their efforts is sticking to one job market or one approach only – e.g. they only apply for online jobs and ignore networking, direct contact and recruitment agencies. To gain maximum results you must aim to utilise all avenues as equally as possible. Of course some may not have the confidence or capacity to network while others may see applying for external jobs as a waste of time, but spreading your bets across all platforms gives you maximum exposure to the market and therefore the highest chance of success. Again, planning is crucial here, but doing it from the outset will make life much easier than starting when you begin to get somewhere.

Finally, consider your online footprint. You would be surprised at just how much information search engines can dig up about you – information employers can locate just as easily. Studies suggest that up to 80% of employers research prospective candidates online, so pre-empt them by doing a little digging yourself. If you uncover anything you don't like the look of either change it yourself if you have the capacity or contact the website owner and ask them to remove the

Planning from the outset is key. Keep a record of what you have sent to whom and when. This makes follow-up calls much easier to plan and execute.

Try to spread your campaign over as many avenues as possible – network, approach directly, register with agencies and apply for advertised jobs. Spreading your bets will heighten your exposure to the market.

Consider your online footprint. Uncovering information about you is easier for a prospective employer than you think.

content if possible. Out of date or dead pages can remain in search engine caches and can therefore still be accessed for a time afterwards, but the major ones also operate cached page removal services, if you are concerned about this. Of course you can't cover up everything, and employers don't expect you to be an angel, but cleaning up your online act prior to your campaign could avoid some potentially difficult questions later on.

Try searching for your own name and see what comes up. If you see something you don't want potential employers to see, contact the webmaster to see if you can have it removed – unless you can remove it yourself.

"Organising is what you do before you do something, so that when you do it, it is not all mixed up."

A.A Milne

"Don't spread yourself too thin. Learn to say no politely and quickly."

St. Francis de Sales

"Around 43% of employers said what they had seen on social networking sites had caused them not to hire the candidate."

CareerBuilder.co.uk Survey, Jan 2010

Chapter 8 – Your CV & covering letter

Your CV and covering letter package is your personal sales pitch and its aim is to get you to the first stage of the recruitment process, be that an interview, a meeting or a simple phone conversation with the company or agency in question. For many however, writing or updating a CV and covering letter is an unpleasant or even daunting task. Knowing what to include, what to leave out and how to phrase everything succinctly, yet with an impact, leaves many wondering just where to start. This may especially be the case for someone who hasn't needed to update their CV for some time.

Put together a list of companies, research them and contact the relevant department with your CV and covering letter. Mention any gaps in the company you may have found during your research that you think you can fill.

This section looks at the CV and the covering letter individually and should help you get a basic idea of how to go about creating a winning application package.

Covering letter

A covering letter is read before a CV and should act as an incentive for the reader to want to read your CV. If the covering letter makes no impression they may not even get that far. Like the CV, this document should be tailored to the job and should reflect but not mirror what is stated in your CV. Mention one or two of your highest and most relevant achievements to impress the reader – don't hide them away in your CV.

A covering letter is read before a CV, so ensure that it makes an impression – otherwise they may not even get to your CV!

Start your covering letter by saying why you are writing and, if you are responding to a vacancy, how you came across it.

The covering letter should start with the obvious – why you are writing to the company. If you don't mention what you want from them how are they going to know? If you are applying for a vacancy, mention how you came to know about it.

Without boasting, say why you are suitable for the position. Mention relevant experience, training and successes.

Next, mention in a couple of sentences why you are the best person for the job. Don't boast, but don't undersell yourself. Mention your experience, training and maybe a star success or two to hook the reader into continuing.

Refer the reader to your enclosed CV and state when you are available for interview.

Refer them next to your enclosed CV and state very clearly when you are available for interview (usually this will be at their 'earliest convenience'). Finally, thank them for their time and consideration and say that you look forward to hearing from them. If posting, ensure also that both the covering letter and CV are in as pristine condition as they can possibly be. All these small factors reflect on your professionalism.

If posting, ensure that your covering letter and CV are stain free!

CV

Whilst there is no single right CV there are plenty of wrong ones out there; rather, there are plenty of mistakes that people make. First and foremost, as I have already discussed, your CV should always be tailored to the type of job and company you had in mind. If you only have one CV which you send to every company regardless of their requirements then you are highly unlikely to hear back from many of them, if any.

There are some common mistakes that people make on their CVs, the most common being neglecting to tailor it to the company and the job in question.

There are typically three types of CV for you to consider. The **performance** CV is the most common and the one you will likely be using yourself. It lists your employment history first, starting with your most recent position, and lists your responsibilities and achievements within those roles. These achievements should be relevant to the company and job you are applying for. Performance CVs are often used by those wishing to remain in the same sector.

*A **performance** CV is most common to those applying for work in their current or most recent sector. It focuses on your positions, roles and responsibilities and runs in chronological order.*

A **skills-based** CV should be used if you have had a varied or broken up career or if you want to change direction. The focus should be on your transferable skills and competencies rather than the companies you worked for and the positions you held. This enables recruiters to see at a glance how your experience and skills match the needs of the job or the company. Consider areas such as team and leadership skills, communication skills, problem solving skills and creative skills.

*A **skills-based** CV is for those who, for whatever reason, have a varied or broken up career. The focus should be on transferable skills which recruiters can match to their requirements.*

Alternative or **portfolio-based** CVs are mainly used by senior managers or those looking for freelance or creative positions. As the name suggests they are usually backed up by a portfolio of work which, to a certain extent, speaks for itself. The CV here acts as a platform for your portfolio and lists achievements during your career.

***Portfolio** CVs are for senior managers, freelancers or those in creative fields and are often supported by a portfolio of work.*

Most employers tend to prefer a two page CV (A4, single sided), but longer CVs are acceptable for specialist positions or where details of managed projects need to be relayed. Academic roles where publications are required to be listed may also require CVs of a longer length. One page CVs are useful for those without much of a career history and may focus more on educational or other related achievements.

Two page CVs are the most common in Britain. However, longer CVs can be used for project management and academic roles.

When it comes to CV layout it really is a personal choice, but there are plenty of templates out there for you to sample. Aside, perhaps, from creative CVs, remember to keep the format sober, professional and uncluttered. Put yourself in the reader's shoes – they are busy people and want to find the key information quickly without having to search for it. Help them out by telling them in an opening paragraph why you want the job and why you would be good for it.

CV templates are available online. Ensure that the format and layout is sober, professional and uncluttered. How easy is it for the recruiter to find the information they will want?

The body of the CV will typically consist of your past jobs, responsibilities and achievements. Don't be tempted to list everything you achieved in all your jobs; only mention your key responsibilities and list only the highlights your prospective employer will find impressive and relevant. Here are some other general points to keep in mind:

List only your key responsibilities and achievements that the recruiter will appreciate.

- Keep your language concise, professional and jargon-free.

- Avoid 'I/my' as in 'I/my revised procedures increased turnover by 75%'. Simply say 'revised procedures increased turnover by 75%'.

- Use the past tense for your career achievements and responsibilities but the present tense for your skills.

- Numbers hold tremendous power. Drop a few impressive statistics into your achievements in number form, ideally mentioning how much money was made or saved as a result, if applicable.

- Avoid writing in capitals, apart from where essential (acronyms etc.).

- Show that you can take the initiative and achieve results. Rather than saying 'supervised the customer service team for retail operations', say 'co-ordinated and led the customer service team to improve satisfaction for retail operations by 29% in six months by harvesting best practices from unrelated industries'.

- Keep the typeface clear and professional. Use a 10-12 point font size in styles such as Times New Roman or Arial and space lines appropriately to avoid cluttering.

Poor spelling and grammar will stick out to a recruiter. If you suspect that these may not be your strong points, ask a trusted friend to have a quick scan for you. There are also numerous CV agencies who will perform this service, as well as giving you further tips and advice.

Use a clear font such as Times New Roman or Arial, point size 10-12 and space lines appropriately to avoid bunching.

Whilst a CV and covering letter alone won't get you a job, they will allow the employer to get a very good idea of who you are and what you may be able to do for them. Make yourself seem perfect for the job and you'll have a very good chance of getting an interview.

Have your CV checked for spelling and grammar by a trusted friend or CV checking organisation.

Finally, don't be tempted to lie on your CV. A good interviewer will question you about many aspects of it, and just one slip up can cause the whole ball of wool to unravel. Lying to get a job means you're trying to make yourself seem ready for something that you're not, and when you have trouble completing tasks your CV says you're a dab hand at, there will only be one result. Climbing the ladder step by step is less risky than jumping for a rung and missing.

A covering letter should be an invitation for the recruiter to read your CV. It should instantly tell them you are the person for the job.

I've learned over the years that when somebody embellishes their resume you don't hire them."

Dick Cheney

"CV's that demonstrated mindset at work and brought it to life just once were three times more likely than others to get the candidate an interview. Those that did it more than once were seven times more likely to get an interview."

James Reed

"It's not as hard to make decisions when you know what your values are."

Roy Disney

Chapter 9 – The interview process

Many of us find interviews extremely unpleasant, which is a situation often made worse if you haven't had an interview for a while. This section offers some advice for helping you through a successful interview and giving you the best chance of success, as well as outlining recent introductions and changes to the recruitment process.

Most of us find interviews unpleasant, especially if we haven't had one for a while.

Research the organisation

The internet has made this much easier to do, so you really have no excuse! A quick visit to the company website, especially the 'about us' section, will give you an overview of their aims, whilst a 'latest news' page should offer up-to-date information on their operations. It wouldn't hurt to jot a few items of the latest news down to repeat at the interview if the chance arises. This shows that you are interested in the company and their direction. A quick online search of the company's name could also throw up some important or interesting information not displayed on the website.

The internet has made researching a company child's play – from their history to their last financial results.

Sharing some interesting information you found whilst researching will show an interest in the company – especially if they have a rich history.

Presentation

As the saying goes, you don't get a second chance to make a first impression. Take the time and effort to turn up well-groomed and in line with the culture of the organisation. If you're not sure of the 'dress code', preferably ask, or just look professional. Arrive five or

Whilst companies may not necessarily have a dress code, it may be worth emulating how existing employees dress.

ten minutes early and announce yourself at reception. You are likely to annoy your host if you arrive too early. Always phone with as much notice as possible if you expect to be delayed. If you can, visit the bathroom to check how you look and take some deep breaths to calm any nerves. Run through your key strengths to yourself whilst you do this. Remember that you are likely to be assessed from the moment you arrive. I recall reading a story in the newspaper recently of a person who went for an interview. After giving her details to the receptionist, she went to a quiet corner of the reception area, called her current employer and suddenly developed a terrible cough, stating that she would be unable to come into work. Needless to say, the receptionist of the potential new employer heard everything and passed the story on to the interviewer.

Arrive early to check you look your best and to calm any nerves. If you anticipate being late, phone as early as possible.

Some employers ask the receptionists for their impressions, so ensure you are polite and professional throughout your waiting time.

Back in reception; meet your interviewer with eye contact, a smile and a confident but not overpowering handshake. These may seem like small details, but a competent interviewer will notice if any are missing and will form an immediate impression of you. If you look good and appear confident you're off to a good start.

Meet your interviewer with a firm handshake, a smile and, crucially, eye contact. These small details don't go unnoticed.

Make an impact

Given the fact that you are being interviewed, someone within the company obviously thinks you have the potential to fulfil the role. Your job in the

Your job is to convince the interviewer that you tick all the boxes they require.

interview is to not only confirm this but, if possible, go beyond that. To start, know your CV inside out. Forgetting or mistaking roles, duties and dates of employment will make you look unprofessional and may lead the interviewer to query further areas of your CV for errors.

Know your CV inside out. Any glaring discrepancies will not look good.

In an interview, you are aiming to stand out from the competition, and there is no better way to do this than to show that you have already successfully performed some of the duties required of you in previous jobs. To this end, have some stories and specific examples up your sleeve where you have encountered, and successfully remedied, similar situations to those anticipated in the role, including any unforeseen benefits (profits, repeat business etc.).

Have up your sleeve a couple of stories where you successfully negotiated similar incidents to those in the job you are interviewing for.

The interviewer won't expect you to know the entire company history, number of staff in the building and the financial projections for the next quarter, but showing that you have researched a little of their history, their aims, what they do and who their competition is will show you are interested in the company as a whole and not just the job. Don't bamboozle them with facts and figures though, and only provide them when appropriate.

Don't relay the entire Wikipedia entry for the company, but make sure you know a bit about the company's history, industry, aims and competitors.

Finally, it never hurts to bring a couple of props to show off your work. This can include a handbook for a project you worked on, a training manual you put

Keep your answers concise and to the point without appearing short. Rambling through answers and avoiding the question won't instil your interviewer with confidence.

together – anything in fact that relates to the job you're interviewing for that will make a positive impression.

Less is more

Try to keep your answers as concise and to the point as possible, but without coming across as curt. How you answer the question reflects how you work and you want the interviewer to see you as someone who gets the job done thoroughly, professionally and with a minimum of fuss. Over talking, especially off the topic in hand, displays a lack of focus and a possible tendency to mentally wander. Structured answers without waffling work best.

Nerves

Interviewers will expect you to be at least a little bit nervous, but over anxiety can represent a concern to them – as can over confidence. A reasonable interviewer however, will always cut you some slack as far as nerves go. If you find the nerves taking over (heart thumping, shaking, sweating) you can always ask for a glass of water. Take a deep breath before each answer (pass it off as careful consideration) and focus on talking slowly, pronouncing each word and taking regular small breaths where needed to avoid gabbling entire sentences. Ensure you maintain eye contact as much as possible, but without staring. A smile now and again doesn't hurt either. If in any doubt, try mirroring

If appropriate, bring in props such as a handbook or portfolio of a project you worked on or a training manual you put together – anything relevant to the job that will help sell you.

All interviewers anticipate nerves, but try to avoid over anxiety.

If you start to feel overly nervous, ask for a glass of water if one isn't offered, take deep breaths before giving your answers and concentrate on delivering your responses.

Maintain eye contact without staring and don't forget to smile.

the expressions and actions of your interviewer. This is a known method of helping someone to relate to you.

Questions

Many people overlook the power of asking questions. Searching, but relevant questions will show that you have researched the position, the company and the market in which it operates. Researching the company will, more often than not, throw up some questions which, combined with anything you want to know about your own position and opportunities, will show that you are interested about wider aspects of the company than just your welfare.

Searching, but relevant questions from you to the interviewer will reinforce your interest in the role and your research into the company.

As well as traditional face-to-face interviews, other forms of assessment are used which are worth mentioning (you may be exposed to a combination of them through one recruitment process):

Other forms of interview often take place in contemporary recruitment processes.

Assessment centres will involve you spending some time with other candidates going through a series of assessments such as interviews, case studies, group and role-playing exercises. These test your teamwork, analytical and leadership skills and feel more relaxed than standard interviews, although you will be monitored throughout.

Assessment centres involve spending time with other candidates completing team oriented and role-playing tasks and interviews.

Psychometric tests are usually written but sometimes verbal tests that offer employers an insight into your characteristics and methods of working. They often include aptitude (verbal, numerical, abstract, spatial,

Psychometric tests offer employers insights into your characteristics and ways of working. They employ a variety of questionnaires and tests to reveal thought patterns.

mechanical) and personality analysis questionnaires, usually with a mixture of free response (your own words), multiple choice (several options) or forced choice (two options) answers. There are inexpensive yet valuable books available to help you prepare for psychometric tests.

In **performance-based tests** you are assessed on how well or quickly you can perform certain tasks. They include tests of attainment (maths, spelling or typing tests or tests of specialist knowledge), ability (verbal, numerical or special tests) and aptitude (how quickly you can pick up new skills).

Whatever test or interview you undertake, try to make sure that you leave the interviewer with the impression that you are professional, keen and dedicated. You know you are the right person for the job – all you have to do is let them know.

Performance-based tests examine how well and quickly you perform certain mental and physical tasks.

Whatever your method of assessment, try to ensure that the employer leaves with a positive view of you and that you do what you can to stand out from the crowd.

"Concentration is a fine antidote to anxiety."

Jack Nicklaus

"So many people out there have no idea what they want to do for a living, but they think that by going on job interviews they'll magically figure it out. If you're not sure, that message comes out loud and clear in the interview."

Todd Bermont

"Not knowing enough about the company or position, displaying a bad attitude or inquiring about compensation prematurely can all leave a negative impression with hiring managers."

Max Messer

Chapter 10 – Case studies

The following real-life case studies illustrate how people in three very different situations accepted change and dealt with it in a way that ultimately proved positive to their careers and wellbeing.

Claudia's story

I had been with a telecoms organisation for 18 months as head of HR. With the overseas parent company looking at flotation, a new HR Director was brought in to manage the process and ensure the organisation could hold up to the scrutiny and rigours of due diligence. A few months later, I was asked to attend a meeting with my immediate boss at our Bristol office. At this meeting we were informed that the layers of HR staff were to be reduced and as such my post was now redundant. I had already wondered how the new HR structure would work, but I was shocked that this meeting was the first (and only) discussion on the subject and wasn't in fact a discussion but a 'fait accompli'. I felt let down, angry and unappreciated. It simply wasn't fair. I was offered paid notice and a lump sum and didn't feel I had any recourse to challenge the decision. My experience of managing the redundancy of other people counted for little, and I felt totally deflated. It was all very personal and entirely out of my control. With the benefit of hindsight, I realise I was rather politically naïve when the new boss had talked to me as part of his induction; I think I had been too honest about my views on HR and he may have seen me as disruptive.

The embarrassment of having to go in and collect my possessions was terrible, as was telling people I had been made redundant. The suddenness of the process really knocked my self-confidence, but as time went on I sought out colleagues and professional support and this helped me move on.

I ended up being out of work for about six months. During this time I reassessed what I wanted out of a job and what new skills I needed to acquire to achieve my new aims. I took a number of short summer courses at my local college and met lots of new people, deciding eventually to do an MBA to broaden my HR skills. Shortly afterwards, I was contacted by a head-hunter about a HR Directorship role. I interviewed and was not only offered the post but also offered funding for my MBA on a part-time basis. I now run my own business which specialises in executive coaching and coaching supervision, leadership team development and board effectiveness. I think my own experience of being made redundant really helped me understand the pressures that today's executives face and the benefits of taking hold of your own career planning. Although it was a painful process, it offered me the chance to proactively manage my career, which I otherwise would not have been able to do. In the long-term it certainly worked out for the better.

Sharon's story

As children, we are all asked what we want to do when we grow up. And for as long as I can remember, my response was always "be a journalist". I remember watching the BBC news whilst still at school, thinking, "That's it. That's what I want to do." After finishing my journalism degree I moved to London and worked my way up through the ranks of a national newspaper, remaining with the same company for five happy years until a strange thing happened: I didn't want to do it anymore. The odd hours, missing Christmases with my family, the tiny salary—what was once the dream had become the reality, and it failed to meet my expectations. After covering the financial crisis of 2008 first hand, I knew I wanted to enter the world of financial services marketing and communications. As with news, I could still learn something new every day and hone my craft, but I'd also have the ability to spend holidays with my family. But I was basically starting my career over from scratch. Where was I to begin?

I started by seeking out friends and acquaintances who worked in similar positions, asking them about what they loved and hated about their jobs. No topic was off the table—this was a major, life-changing decision, and I wanted the nitty-gritty. Of course, there's good and bad with every job, but I wanted to know if the good was good enough to counteract the bad. I was very lucky in that people were willing to be very candid with me. And once I got the answers I needed, I knew I was ready to make the switch.

My next challenge was to translate the skills I'd gleaned from one field as being the perfect fit for my new career. After learning more about what it took to succeed in financial marketing and communications, I honed in on a few key links and put these items on paper as bullets on my resume and points in my cover letter, as well as asking the friends I had spoken to, to be referees on my behalf. Rather than ignoring my resume because I didn't have a traditional background, I found that employers were curious about my career path and why I was making a change. And after telling my story and confirming my qualifications, I found that most places were eager to have a fresh perspective in the office.

After networking (a lot!) and many, many conversations with potential employers, I secured my first job in my career restart. A completely new field also brought a new learning curve however, and I thought it would be a good idea to increase my knowledge about the marketing world. I didn't want to take on any student loan debt, so I opted for part-time education, working during the day and going to class at night. Yes, this was a big commitment, but the supplementary expertise helped me get up to speed more quickly, made me a better asset to my new team, and—as a bonus—gave me greater confidence that I was right where I belonged.

Dominic's story

I had worked in the competitive and highly pressurised arena of corporate consulting for a blue chip multinational. I was feeling burnt out after 25 years focusing on profit making companies and felt that the time was right for me to give something back.

With the help of a career change organisation I focused on my areas of personal interest, the work/life balance I was now looking for and fulfilling my need of doing something for the greater good. I then undertook a skills inventory which included:

- My ability to meet ever changing needs

- Excellent communication and interpersonal skills

- A well-honed resilience working within time-critical environments

- Proven team player – a natural collaborator

- Having a persuasive and confident nature

- Extensive knowledge and business contacts within blue chip organisations

- A can do attitude, with an ability to communicate at all levels

- Solution-focussed, adept at problem solving

- Key skills in supporting and motivating a team

- Capable of seamlessly integrating into new environments

My career counsellor and I focused on common denominators which could be packaged well to prospective employers, in particular, the charity sector where I was sure I wanted to move into. My existing skills were perfect in marketing myself to charities for corporate fundraising positions. Through coaching assignments I was able to target the charities I most wanted to work for and speculatively approached contacts I had researched from my wish list. Within nine weeks I had two face-to-face interviews, three telephone conversations with senior individuals within three different charities, and was then offered my dream job for one of the UK's leading charitable organisations.

An important aspect of my experience was that these job opportunities were not advertised – I created my own desired outcome with the support and guidance of my career coach.

Conclusion

The twin aims of this handbook have been to provide you with an insight into the future of the employment landscape and also to help you navigate this landscape in order to ensure that you either remain a valuable asset to your chosen organisation, or, if you wish to change your career focus, that you can offer value to one of the growing industries outlined in the book. As the pace of the world increases so does the pace of the change within it, and hopefully this book has shown you where this change is headed in the forthcoming years, and how to adapt to it. A career nowadays lasts for some fifty years, and you only have to look back over the last fifty years to see just how the world of work has changed in that time. Working for fifty years is a hard slog there's no doubt about it, and now, more than ever before, we have to be open to the prospect of change if we want to be successful at what we do, regardless of whether we are driven by personal success, the need or desire to provide for others or happiness in our lives.

The organic and fluid nature of the working world, however, means that this book should not be viewed as the definitive record on what career changes you should make but rather should act as a platform from which you can explore the areas that you feel are of most benefit to you before deciding what action is necessary. For example, some of you will focus on your skill set, while others will feel that further research into the aforementioned growing industries is more pressing. Some of you may have very firm ideas on what you want to do and in what industry but have forgotten how to interview. Each of us is different and will have different priorities, but hopefully this book has given you some insight into what areas of employment you should be investigating and also what skills you need to brush up on in order to ensure that you are fully capable of taking on the roles of the future.

As I mentioned in the introduction, it is our responsibility as career-minded individuals to monitor changes in employment and industry and to act accordingly.

This doesn't mean making regular wholesale changes because of the predictions of one think-tank but instead remaining vigilant – keeping an eye on the fortunes of the industry you are in, for example, or checking job adverts for roles you might consider in the future, to see what types of skills are being sought. These sorts of small, regular activities will ensure that you are better placed than many to ride the waves of change and ensure that you have the skills to meet the demands of the future.

Good luck!

References

1. Claire Macaulay. (2003). *Job Mobility and Job Tenure in the UK*. Office for National Statistics, Labour Market Trends. November 2003, 541-550.

2. Paul Gregg and Jonathan Wadsworth (2011). *The Labour Market in Winter: The State of Working Britain*. Oxford: OUP.

3. CIPD. (2013). *Megatrends: the trends shaping work and working lives*. Available: http://www.cipd.co.uk/binaries/6251%20Megatrends%20(WEB).pdf. Last accessed 6th November 2013.

4. Caitlin Moldvay and Douglas Kelly. (2012). *Dying Industries*. Available: http://www.ibisworld.com/Common/MediaCenter/Dying%20Industries%20final.pdf. Last accessed 6th Jan 2014.

5. Toon Van Beeck. (2011). *Ten Key Industries That Will Decline, Even After the Economy Revives*. Available: http://www.ibisworld.com/Common/MediaCenter/Dying%20Industries.pdf. Last accessed 6th Jan 2014.

6. Ricky Newman. (2012). *10 Businesses That Will Boom in 2020*. Available: http://money.usnews.com/money/careers/articles/2012/09/10/10-businesses-that-will-boom-in-2020. Last accessed 6th Jan 2014.

7. Bureau of Labor Statistics, *Weekly and Hourly Earnings Data from the Current Population Survey*. Washington, DC: US Department of Labor, 2007

8. Anna Davies, Devin Fidler and Marina Gorbis. (2011). *Future Work Skills 2020*. Available: http://www.iftf.org/uploads/media/SR-1382A_UPRI_future_work_skills_sm.pdf. Last accessed 6th Jan 2014.

9. James Reed and Paul G Stoltz (2013). *Put Your Mindset to Work: The One Asset You Really Need to Win and Keep the Job You Love*. London: Penguin.

10. Kevin Kruse. (2012). *Top 4 Traits of "Future Proof" Employees, According to 1,709 CEOs*. Available: http://www.forbes.com/sites/kevinkruse/2012/12/26/ibm-ceo-study/. Last accessed 6th Jan 2014.

Other Books by Clive Lewis OBE

The Definitive Guide to Workplace Mediation & Managing Conflict at Work

This book is ideal for those seeking to learn more about the concept of mediation in the workplace and the time and money that can be saved by engaging conflict resolution strategies.

Win Win: Resolving Workplace Conflict: 12 Stories

This book presents a series of 12 stories that bring to life tales of difficulty and the role played by the author as a mediator and dispute resolution specialist. This book will be of benefit to anyone dealing with workplace conflict.

Difficult Conversations – 10 Steps to Becoming a Tackler not a Dodger

In life you are either a tackler or a dodger. This easy read book provides you with 10 simple steps to boost your skills and confidence allowing you to tackle, not dodge that difficult conversation.

Order form

Looking for Your Next Job?

Work: Where to find it and how to get hired.

Book Quantity	Price
1-14 copies	£9.99 each
15-29 copies	£7.99 each
30-99 copies	£5.99 each
100-999 copies	£5.75 each
1,000-4,999 copies	£5.50 each
5,000-9,999 copies	£5.25 each
10,000 or more copies	£5.00 each
ebooks – per book	**Price**
	£6.99

Name: .... Job Title: ....

Organisation: ....

Address: ....

Postcode: .... Tel No: ....

Email: ....

(Postage and packing £3 – please contact Globis for multiple or overseas purchases)
☐ Cheque enclosed (Please make payable to Globis Ltd)
☐ Please invoice *(only if over £100)*
☐ Please debit my credit card

Name on Card: .... Card Number: ....

Start Date: .... Expiry Date: .... Security No: ....

Signed: ....

Post completed form to: Globis Ltd, Unit 1, Wheatstone Court, Quedgeley, Gloucester GL2 2AQ

Tel: 0330 100 0809
Fax: 01452 726001
Email: info@globis.co.uk

About the author

Clive Lewis OBE is a leading employee relations and dispute resolution specialist, facilitator, coach, trainer, author and speaker. He is founding director of the Globis Mediation Group, and an accredited commercial mediator specialising in helping to solve complex one on one, team, organisational, multiparty and collective disputes. He is the author of four books including *The Definitive Guide to Workplace Mediation', 'Win Win: Resolving Workplace Conflict: 12 Stories'* and *'Difficult Conversations – 10 Steps to Becoming a Tackler not a Dodger'* as well as numerous published articles on mediation in the workplace. His work has taken him across three continents and has included advising governments outside the UK.

In addition to his day job, he is a non-executive director in the NHS and a Trustee of the National Youth Jazz Orchestra. He is also founder of Bridge Builders Mentoring, a not-for-profit delivering mentoring to pupils from poor socio economic backgrounds. His commitment to charity work led to him being appointed as Chair of a government appointed independent panel exploring the rising costs of youth underachievement. In 2011 he was awarded the OBE for public service and was commissioned as a Deputy Lieutenant in 2012.

Notes Page

Notes Page

Notes Page

Clive Lewis